POEMS

Little God

AVNI VYAS

BURROW PRESS | ORLANDO, FL

PRAISE FOR...

"Part trickster, part soulmate, part self-reflection, there is nothing small about Avni Vyas's little god, a tart and clever figure who begets fragments, windy seasons, and littler gods, words he wants to make and perform."
–**Anne Barngrover**, author of B*razen Creature*

"Welcome to the world, Little God. You're the book we all need. Avni Vyas roars and soars in this important debut, reminiscent of Marquez's idea that 'All human beings have three lives: public, private, and secret.' It's that secret life that tugs at us, and Vyas gets to the core—to the heartbeat of this wanting, in this litany of 'almosts' filled with claws, filled with teeth—filled with heartbeat after heartbeat. This book is a wonder. It sings a storm. Most importantly, it makes us consider the root of all our longing—no one does this like Vyas."
–**Dorothy Chan**, author of *BABE*

"Ornery and opinionated, the character of Little God adopts the childish and critical voice in readers' heads, "suss[es] out [our] mopes," and, in the cage of Avni Vyas's mouth, where words rattle and echo with sumptuous abandon, taunts and teases us into submission. The way only a mean love can, Little God makes us see ourselves—bruised, smelly, and deserving of forgiveness. This is a thrilling landscape of loss, love, and language that begs to be read aloud after a cocktail to anyone who will listen. And, believe me, they will."
–**S. Whitney Holmes**,
author of *Room Where I Get What I Want*

...LITTLE GOD

"In this dazzling debut of a collection, Avni Vyas asks the important not often considered question: What if our gods aren't malevolent or benevolent, but like…just kind of annoying? Churlish and childish figures who poke us when we're trying to concentrate on the act of living, who blow in our ears right at the most important part of the movie, or fart under the covers right before we get in. Vyas explores the shadow grief of what-ifs and lives almost lived, and through her keen sense of humor and stunning pathos, she reveals to us how we can be our own gods. Sure, hers is a little mischievous and totally exhausting, but also loving, and perhaps most importantly, forgiving. Let her Little God sit on your shoulder, cackle, and slap his knee next time you stumble and falter through life's most important moments. Vyas shows us here – he's teaching you something."
–**Nik De Dominic**, author of *Your Daily Horoscope*

"Little God is our deejay through the miasma of time. Listen, you believers and everyone else, too. Little God will save your poetic soul."
 –**Barbara Hamby**, author of *Holoholo*

"Each of us has a little god, someone who knows you better than you know yourself. He's your pal, though you're never quite sure what he's up to. But isn't that what you want? Our little gods delight and edify us, as do these smart, needle-sharp poems."
–**David Kirby**, author of *More Than This*

©Avni Vyas, 2021
All rights reserved.
Published by Burrow Press
burrowpress.com

Cover & Illustrations: Mimi Cirbusova
Book Design: Ryan Rivas
POD Edition
ISBN: 978-1-941681-15-2

for my family

A NOTE TO THE READER

Thank you for spending time with the poems in this collection. Your time and attention are valuable gifts, and I am thankful you choose to spend them with poetry.

The events leading up to writing *Little God* in my personal life inform the collection as a whole: For most of 2019, my father's health existed in a medical limbo where my family and I hoped, prayed, and waited. In October of the same year, my partner Matthew and I learned we were pregnant. As my family braced for multiple possible futures, Matt and I protected the pregnancy as a kind of secret, psychic buoy to embrace through uncertainty. When the ultrasound revealed no heartbeat, my panic around my father's health finally focused on my own. Many people write about how lonely miscarrying can be. It is. However, these poems are not about that event, but the poems are informed by this loss.

These events in my current life echoed events from a past life: a previous loss, this time a relationship, an earlier *almost*. During the composition of *Little God*, these *almosts* threaded across the poems, pointing to past or possible lives that one could imagine, but not live. In this way, the *almost* lives became more possible to consider in conversation, which became possible by shifting my attention to receiving, listening. The *almosts* became gods.

Imagine meeting the most forlorn, implacable version of yourself, and treating them like a deity. Like many desi kids, I grew up with stories of Lord Krishna's childhood. His pudgy, blue face beamed from wall calendars and prints in my family's home. Part innocent life-force, part coddled brat, the figure of a child god appealed to me as a writing partner. In this spirit, the poems in *Little God* are collaborative and conversational.

The poems in *Little God* were composed ambidextrously. I alternated between composing with left and right hands to draft these poems. I hoped that composing with my non-dominant hand would allow for a different relationship to language and text production. What I learned surprised me: poems written in my non-dominant hand were often more tender in tone, gentler, somehow—a necessary balance to the sharp grief my dominant hand was writing.

You should know I'm left-handed. I prefer to write in graph paper composition books in fine, ballpoint ink. You should know my handwriting is my favorite physical feature. I'm even vain about it: Distinctive and efficient, its tiny spikes and loops, from a distance, appear to be a font. I take notes when I'm out in the world, and I like how my thoughts arrive in ink. Most of all, I like how the words form a seam from the page to the pen and back to me, a sacred circuit. Adapting writing constraints around composing longhand means changing the circuitry of how I access language. Embracing the spooky, ragged scrawl of my non-dominant hand reminded me again of the patience writing requires.

I noticed the poems composed by my dominant (left) hand performed poetry. The lyric leap, image, and surprise worked predictably to form, at times, a hermetic insularity. In contrast, my right-handed poems were often simpler, but more tender in sentiment. At first the sentiment embarrassed me, but soon the earnest, imperfect script looked like my dad's handwriting in the hospital. Unable to speak or type, he focused his energy one night to document what he thought might be his final night. In my right-handed scrawl, I could see him, hear my past in the voice of an angry child, feel the weight of my ex's shame and disappointment. In this way, the right-handed poems afforded a more direct conversation between grief and comfort.

I said, "Don't touch my mouth. There's ~~teeth~~ in there,"

and you replied,

"There's ~~teeth~~ everywhere on you."

Today that little, holy god-scrap trampled my bras and chewed apart my underwear

The majority of these poems were written as part of an annual monthly poem-a-day practice with a group of poets I respect and admire. With these skilled and kind poets as my first readers, I felt encouraged to commit to the strangeness of the project. As the poems collected throughout the month, it was clear that the purpose of the poems was to invite conversation, or play. My left-handed poems stopped gritting their teeth quite so tightly. My right-handed poems started flossing their fangs. Rather than opposition or binaries, the ambidextrous composition invites arcs, beats, back-and-forth, a landing.

—AVNI VYAS
MARCH 2021

LITTLE GOD SPEAKS DOG

At first you smell like plastic bags
and stale cardboard, a sad sweat
older than you, rose, pepper.

When I smell you again, I can suss out
your mopes (My jaws clamp it!
It's in your arms! Your legs snake with it!)

and for a few days, your skin blossoms
with tender spots (Your sad?
I killed it?) but your smell shifts.

Clay, grubs. I watch the blues
climb out of you to eat the sun.
I watch it grow. I snap the necks
of what sprouts in your garden,

lest it remind you of the un-sun,
the night invaded by white heads
glowing on iron stakes, or after

we trek for miles until you smell like yourself,
and I want to lick it off you. Be your rain.

Want to breathe you, grow you,
madden, toughen, spin you. Please,

smell how much I want to be alive with you.

Today I love
the little god
who begets
fragments:

of the time
in workshop
when William
held his hand
hovering, pledging

for two whole
sentences
as he spoke
of his beloved
before noticing us
watching.

Of Ekalavya
slicing off
his thumb
as an oath
to never
best his guru.

Of *prestidigitation*,
a word I could rattle in my
mouth's cage for an hour.

Of weighted blankets.

Of a coach's twang
caroming
in my head
for 200 meters.

Of your silver
hoops. How when you'd

flick the left one,
and a high E rang out

like a dropped glass,
a shriek.

Today the little god
wants his fortune told,
so I fake it:

*Your crown will be frosted
in epiphytic pups.*

*You'll receive fresh cleats
with gold-tipped toes.*

*A storm cracks during prayer,
and lightning will ooze
against a sky gone milky.*

You'll have answers.

*You'll eat light with your eyes,
devour libraries.*

*Forgiveness will arrive as
a gust from the revolving
border between temple and street.*

Today the god
drains his offerings

(a shot of rum,
a minneola tangerine,
an almond)

but resists
being slaked.

Light vaults into the pond
past the mass of fish nests
where minnows shimmer

in small blades.

The god asks why I am
so slow to forgive.

Why I hold,
unmelted,
your old rock.

Are you helping, the god asks,
the atoms unearth?

He slaps his tiny,
god-sized knee.

Are you helping,
tears of laughter
rolling now, *anything at all?*

Today that
little holy
god-scrap

trampled
my bras
and chewed
apart my
underwear

in a prayer-
sanctioned
assemblé,
a numbskulled
namaskara,
tatta adavu
bharatnatyam
from before.

In tatters,
I chased him,
my body useless,
a soft bell
with no clapper
and he was
delighted.

The little god wants
to make words.

He demands
to know why,
when I flip
the magazine
to a page
of a bright
green lawn
—an ad for fertilizer—

WHY,
in all his days,
haven't I ever
taken him there—

He interrupts himself with
a parade of ants

—a thread the god follows,

ribboning from room to room,

blessing the creatures
and their shadows—

that bobs up through
a crack in the wall.

The godlet
contemplates leaving.

You would miss me too much, he says.

*You'd live off saltines and boiled
peanuts. Ugh, your claws.
I'll stay.*

LITTLE
GOD
EXPLAINS
DOGS

You worry
that the dogs
leaking from
your neighbors'
porous fences
may frighten me,

("Is this a sign? The fuel of
poetic intransigence?")

but dogs are
diplomats of the
underworld, friends
disguised as eviction notices.

You think that
body belongs to you?
Oh, my sun-drunk love,
my spiked lemonade,
you've sanitized yourself
against death. All dogs know

they're born covered
in someone else's blood.

The little god
suggested
not-so-gently

—even his snores
are a windy season—

that the difference
between gods
and demons

is where you let
a spirit live.

Why ferry fire to hell?
he asks. Then:

Can you bring some for me?

Fire? I ask.

No, hell.

I conjure a bowl of heartbreak:

The first shoots
from our garden bed,

a jar of cardamom jam,
cufflinks you were
too ashamed to love.

I tell the god how you fill up
a doorway, presuming solitude,

and the cat escapes under the house
like a tawny flame,

and I chase after her
on all fours:

*LET THERE
BE WARS*,
the god wheezes,

and I emerge,
clotted cobwebs
intact, glaring.

LITTLE WARS!

The cat's mouth devoid
of lizard, eyes wild and moony.

You wanted to leave her
out, let her kill some.

YOU'RE NOT OFF THE HOOK,
the god reminds me.
YOU'RE THE ONE
WHO LOVES WASHING THE DEAD.

Little god
admonishes me
for the times
I didn't waggle it.

He sees the ducks
waggle themselves
and each other.

The whap-flap waggle
of vacationing peafowl,

the pollinated burlesque of
green-scum ponds,

erotica of spiked
scrub palm on pink
silk cotton blossom.

I want to dance
the worm-food waggle,
the pollinator pastiche,
the stupid stamen sonata!

I am delighted.

This bitty smidgen,
his tears drop and explode
like roasting corn.

The god would like to be
instructed on human ululation,
that harvest

of moans

he hears accumulate
like a divine system
both fixed and faraway,
a horizon.

We listen to cows, whales,
wolves call for one another
but it's not the same.

I tell him how
we'd sing "Lilac Wine"
but could never summon
enough mercy.

Turns out gods don't truck in mercy.

I wanted to know mercy,
sure, but I too wanted
to be a god.

Seldom one to apologize,
god-of-everything subatomic

eats right out of my head,
unaware, gnashing

an electronic
hangover.

We could comfort each other
huddled in illness,

and we will,
from separate rooms,
cry each other's stupid credo:

His, to burn in his wake
any spiritual melanoma,

and mine, to conduct
the commerce of
spiritual flagellation.

Our voices
bob through
sunlight
in chorus:
> *I don't need anyone.*
> *I don't need anyone.*

The next time we meet,
the little god arrives in the
recovery room of the abortion clinic

as if he were Catullus
plucking through an underwear
drawer in a strip mall.

The Romans, he swears, *boast
a cup size for every occasion.*

Why not this one?

He finds me drinking Sprite in a recliner splitting
some Goldfish crackers with another woman.

We hold hands.

During the procedure, I fixated:
a doctor complained a nurse signed her name
in the wrong shade of blue ink. *Turquoise is not blue.*

"Blue's blue!"

But he sounded like the little god.
You did this to yourself.

Blue bruises before it reddens,
so I remain unwilling
to translate "It's time to go now"
for my new friend.

("Tienes novio?" "Tengo miedo.")

The little god loved me then. My god,
I thought, bouncing between my hand
and the door. Then, months later, the ringing.

How you said, free as a dart, a vaccine
against my own stupid heart,

"Strange to get you pregnant now
that you've had someone else's abortion."

Like a red-shouldered hawk, the little god
divebombs puddle after puddle in the parking lot,
mistaking the reflection for a depth, a door.

> *Do you remember how we met?*

Yes.

> *Tell it.*

They'd given me meds

> *Called Deathmaker?*

Well, it wasn't called

> *But you called it*

Yes. But because someone else did.

> *Because of Death?*

No, just tissue expulsion

> *That's not death-like enough for you?*

No just that

> *That you didn't die.*

Yes. I got to live.

> *And that's when we met?*

Almost. That's when I remember we'd met before.

> *When you refused English?*

Yes.

> *When we brokered new cuss words!*

Yes.

> *Our shoes were the same size. And you didn't die!*

Legs mottled
beer bottle green,
scratched bite marks

in place of pantyhose
I watch the little god who asks,

What?
What are the rules?

First: let your animal
mark you only once.

Another: whoever snaps the necks
of sunflowers must replace them.

And then the one
I never mastered:

When one of us cries
the secret name
—not the sound
     of the thing
     we are called,

but the howl
from the terrible storm
that beats apart the world—

we follow its command.
Come home. Come home.

What did you do instead,
the little god asks.

I hoarded the silence,
stitched it into a sail,
plugged my ears, fled in the night,
screeched myself mad.

Oh! the god cries.

I forgot the storm can sing!

We're at
each other's
throats.

Before he was
a god, this old
windsock deity

was a ghoul
squatting in my
lower intestine.

The only difference!
Is where!
In the temple!
You house!
The ghost!

Now at home
basking in late
afternoon honeycomb,

the ghoul turns to me
and says,
It was me, you know.
It was me who starved
and strangled you.

Your neck tender
as summer rain.

The god wants to know
The word for
this unending
nowness,

the nights blurred and skinless.
The days, boneless.

Like I'm an idea made from code.
I used to be clay. Cream.

He refuses what I offer.

"Impatience" is floral,
"Eternity" too disrespectful
of deep time, and "tedium,"

just saying it

led him to betrayed tears.

I thought you were going to say
titty, and I love that word.

Doldrums, lassitude,
the supple gone slack.

I wish the nowness
would reveal itself like it does
to me: all day,
wasps daub a hive overhead.

Tomorrow, it will roar.

I tell the god about bobtail squid
who pulse light-bearing

bacteria in an organ
shaped like a cowboy hat

to counter-illuminate
 while hunting at night.

They erase their moonshadows
from the sand floor.

Imagine being mistaken for moonlight.

The god laughs
like dry hair in the winter.

Mistaken?
You poor thing.

LITTLE GOD EXPLAINS COMEDY

When you were born,
you worked the best
party trick in the hospital.

Your lungs,
the size of some
mens' thumbs,
sang a starshine
of bird cries.

And you,
full head
of hair,

gripped by your
newborn fists,

played patsy
to the oldest
joke in history:

grip to come alive;
to stop the pain,
quit.

But since you only
knew the setup,
how could you, little bird,

land it?

So you gripped.
And we wept.

One astrologer
said my chart
sprouted hard angles,
and I required hooves,
horns. The god
thinks star maps
are vouchers

for megalomania.

The banyans, he explains,
voice echoing Herbie Hancock
in the shower,

*are a predatory tree species.
They colonize!*

Who is *they*? I ask.

WE, he says, pointing at his

blue skin glowing from
its own neon feed

WE mangle.

The stars smash, know only to orbit.
I'm tired of artifacting beauty.

Something or nothing, happens.

Dance about it,
he spits.

I dance you into a corner,
        roll wild azalea buds
                in my cupped palm, their rattle

a kind of anxious mating call
        not of azaleas or gods, but
                of geometry,

an order in the eventual
        flimsy unfolding of
                a map, its continents

vast and familiar
        as our own organs,
                marked oceans, safe harbors,
        and over there, coils of fins and spume

so monstrous and electric that
        I could destroy the blue
circuitry holding me intact,

that you won't let me
        dance it alone.

The god abdicates
from dancing as the

ring-of-flame bearer

when he discovered
Saturn ate his own son.

His own father
beheaded him
as his mother bathed,
so the wound smarts.

*What happens
when we eat
our young?* he asks,
poison jaws
gleaming.

They claw out, I say.

The god would
never—here, he
holds my delicious,
blazing face—
consume and forget
like that. He has

your eyes the night
you begged to stay,

and our howls rang
hollow inside
the other's temple.

When I punk out
on myself droning
litanies of almosts,
the god, bored,
haunts someone else.

I should be jealous
but a part of me knows
it takes skill to
run off a god.

Yesterday, the spoonbills
scattered their pink
felicitations
          somewhere else.

It is late afternoon
before you arrived
in my thoughts as

the water buffalo
whose rampage
razed an ashram
where Shiva, eons
deep in tapasya

barely felt the temple
walls crack.

Tethered to the village
by a Brahmin curse,
the buffalo gored the banyan
before resting in its shade.

Maybe the god's gone
somewhere better, like

community beach yoga
by the experimental
donut shop, tie-dyed
cotton cover-ups,
dizzy columns
of juice and booze,
enough investment
jewels to live off for years,

but I imagine him here,
glowering, marking
the edge
of the sentiments
"you know me"
       and
"you don't know me,"

the way you'd coax me
from one ledge
to another, feigning
knowing,

the only trick
that lured me back:

"Of course I know you."

How a panhandler's
earnings double
as alms and a grift.
Me, pockets empty,
begging to get ripped off.

LITTLE
GOD
ATTENDS
COMMUNITY
BEACH
YOGA

I learn about letting go
from white people chanting *om*.

If I watch the ocean in downward dog,
the birds stand single-legged,
resting between bursts of sky.

If I don't, carpenter ants find us
this side of the dunes. Meanwhile,
the clouds smack their gum, whack
open the shutters of rental homes
to reveal seashell art, soft blue couches,
cartoon wine bottles, single-use
soap coins, stiff hand towels,
a guest book full of bleached pages.

Then, they set me loose
in the Gulf, waving their sails at my farewell.

It only makes sense to head home fast.

A nice sound, *home*.

Wonder what language it's reminding me of.

My future
glitters
with new gods:

One scalds tongues
if you eat too fast.

Another stokes
a jacuzzi all night

in case traveling
snowbirds need to party.

My favorite boasts
your chin, sharp as
a tin-can punch.

He devours confusion
as an offering

and attends to squeaking
door hinges.

He wants devotion.

They all do.

The future can't eliminate wanting

so instead we sing karaoke,
wipe down our surface
defects with good light, houseplants.

Best chew the gravel
of ourselves to
to simulate fullness.

A manatee god
replaces the little one
with a string
of jokes:

Have you ever noticed

how manatees,
when they overtake you
in the passing lane,
bob along like the children
of boulders
and baked potatoes?

Manatees are mermaids
with great personalities,
he says. He whips up a
mean risotto, never once
comparing me
to an emotional support
sweater. Slowly

I peel back
the curtain
from my true form,

        a sea creature couplet of

song and silence,
lung and gill, a

tumescent glowing
orb to lure him with.

He covets my
psychic graffiti,
boasts it on his scarless hide.

This is the animal that scares me most:

the promise my straying
         was a one-off, as if I had not
been stashing scarves and books
         back into my suitcase for years.

Did you notice I barely moved in?

How, if I slipped a garbage bag
         over the heads of my hangers,

I could zip up and fly off any morning?

I left notes
         (PLEASE LOVE ME, I'M EVAPORATING),
taped them to the fridge, the vertical
         scrawl of uncertain affections.
         I loved you in hallways with weak light.
I loved you like an angry orange soda
         street light on the corner of Branch Street

         (PLEASE, DO YOU SENSE IT?)

outside the bedroom where,
    naked, you boasted on either cheek,
temporary tattoos, a gift from the
    latest makeshift beloved,

and then I remember how once I learned to play
    "Please please please (Let Me Get What I Want)"
and you said, "It's not my favorite, but it's good," so

I hate myself in this poem.

I should push her out a window
    before she reveals her wingspan,
her pelican throat.

The little god is unimpressed. He lounges
    in your office on a pink inflatable couch,
crinkling Tofutti Cutie wrappers.

On his way out, he traces my script,
    as tiny and vast as the red ant colony's tunnels
bleeding apart your walls.

He's off to circle the artificial thermals from
    a wastewater plant's mean fumes,

waiting for it to get worse.

A storm blows
the little god back in.
He nests in my hair,
a battered crown
softly glowing.

My dreams taste like stale limes.

Waking, he asks for coffee
and explains my karmic
failures with an
itemized list:
vanity, a cloud

of starlings.
Pride, a weak
frozen daiquiri.

Did you meet other gods
out there? I ask.

Only ghosts, he says, *acting like gods.*

Terrible outfits,
disappointing, he says,
adjusting his ski mask.

Ducks prefer
a semaphore of feathers
(that's cute)
but he carves me into
an escape hatch.
He, a near-conquered
predator, licks his claws,

zips into a skinsuit.

Now I'm your heartbeat,
your allergies, your passwords.
I glue soft talons of eyelashes to my face.

When I try too hard,
I blink your heart open, and
burgle your whole kingdom.

Where were you?

> *You didn't need me*

Bullshit.
I was miscarrying
a whole past
and a possibility.

> *You were digesting yourself*

Yeah, you drip. I was.

> *Honestly? It was a chore to witness*
>
> *You insist on beating it against*
> *the rocks of each river you travel*

It?

> *What else to call*
> *unproven notions?*
> *An embryo, a child?*
>
> *You were sloughing off*
> *your futures. Molting.*
>
> *I was on the other side of the dressing room.*

You broke into my house
while I slept.

> *And I looked like everyone you ever lost.*

When the duckling,
—more like duck,
more like business
lunch, like unfettered
petty cash—

dismounts on the balcony,
the little god's already
wheeling and dealing.

They trade for the day

and the god flaps off
while the duck
roosts as a god.

They're all gods, the duck says.
Everyone you bring inside.

I'm sick of fixating,
but the duck says no,
stay here. Feel it,

the heart unraveling open
from loving someone else,

its bright shock of rope
unspooling where it couldn't before,
whole arms,
stretches to leap,

how supple
the new distance,

to un-god and re-god as needed.
To need.

The god sets
my brain ablaze
with steel drums
acid-plinking
their way
up and down
the scales.
Sunshine, a lace
of shadows, minor
keys, bells.

We're levitating,
though it's more
like treading water,
muscles furious
and contained like
a cruel smile.

Perhaps in a future,
your hands float
ready to conduct
an orchestra of
outrage-and-vinegar.

And thus we stay
afloat in a whelm,
a heartbeat paradox.

As long as you're a figment,
I go on kicking underwater.

The little god
begets littler gods.

How the Greeks did it—

What, myth? Wars?

He wants a temple
guarded by wolves
but I counter-offer:
A swamp full of lizards.

I'm not that type of god.

Except he is. His hog-
grunts of dissent.
Sunning his wares,
mouth half-open,
an eye or foot torn off.

Gods sprout
from those absences
in petals, moons
glowing in their centers.

At night the swamp
out-sings the traffic.

We fill ourselves on cicadas.

The god weaves his shrine
where I demand a place
inside to place a heart or stump.

LITTLE
GOD
DISCOVERS
SLANG

It started as a joke, calling yourself *thiccboi*
    ("Two c's for showmanship!") and slid
its parlance to mean "little fish" or "faraway bird."

Under a bridge, thicc pelicans slurping thiccie minnows.
    Soon crabs and lizards became thiccies,
fat flashes of life rolling like gas station hot dogs

before they're plucked off. Thicc nimbuses
    mating over this thicc mangrove forest.
Taking on lives of their own, your thiccies

wrest themselves into a dictionary of uses
    or else bob like buoys we can always reach.
Thiccboi ocean. Thicc motorboats. Thiccer still,

the light, burled from gold-honey to amber-blood,
    and in that red, the swarm of all we have been carrying,
tiny magnitudes coalesced into thicc beloveds.

For our first date,
you collect me
from the airport
with an avocado
and hot sauce.

Like the score to a
grand-juried blockbuster
about best friends in love,

you drive your pickup
under an abandoned mansion,
where we excise with tenderness
the fruit's spicy flesh from its skin.

Later, kissing in the main cab,
I think about how
your hands cradle animals
during euthanasia.

Your left hand steady,
my skull floating.

I said, "Don't
touch my mouth.
There's teeth in there,"

and you replied,

"There's teeth
everywhere
on you."

In Florida, the sun enacts its laws.
The male carp nudge circles of silt
into mating nests with slick, red fins.

No need to tousle
our fears further, but we know
we're swaddled in one

long goodbye we hope
drags out with our lives
entwined, surviving.
Today, we watch fish, drink coffee.

I want to know I belong
to this wanting and carrying on.

I want to be there with you,
when your son looks outside, his face
a blue-white wordless weather.

The shower
buzzes like
a bell's hollow
and I soap my legs
with executive
affection so
stubble, nick,
and seam teem
in the same cloud.

*Eventually, the future
shows up everywhere.*

Soon, I'm all of it:
bulb, acid, pith,
soldered human
clump of
then, *now,* and *soon*.

One day, you'll be gone
but for now,
you and the god
fill everything:

earworm of ambulance sirens,
wasps nesting, a low
rumble of rainstorms

like an abused
piano. The god
pounds our heavy
strings because
he loves their echoes.

LITTLE GOD SINGS FOR THE UNBORN

Though you never made it to
this side of the underworld,
know I dream of you
as my sister.

Even now, you share my wardrobe,
teach me the cold blade of a
well-placed, "So what?"

You slip whiskey in my cola,
calculate a real bra size, lament
hair-glitter, man-buns, animal cruelty.

You draw a bath and say,
"Haven't you seen a woman
love herself before?"
when you know I haven't.

I hear you mock my dates at family dinner,
hissing, "Now what?"

You wait for me in the bathroom mirror,
wearing our face on its silver surface,
until I say, "We become, my bird."

ACKNOWLEDGEMENTS

Bottomless thanks to my personal pantheon:

to Geeta, Janak, and Raju Vyas, and my extended family for a lifetime of love and support

to Dano Moreno, Eva Fiallos-Diaz, and Paco Fiallos for their continuous emotional and creative generosity, including video messages of solidarity and encouragement

to Emily Carr and Nick Clarkson for their expansive creative and collegial friendships

to Deanna Zastrow and Andrew Mayronne for countless vent sessions, pep talks, and teaching me resilience

to Jennifer Wells, Allie Maass, Andrea Kneis, and Amy Wallace for their haven of friendship and community

to the PAD crew: Michelle Burke, Carrie Chappell, Nik DeDominic, Brett Evans, Jeremy Allan, Hawkins, Whitney Holmes, Justin Runge, Benjamin Sutton, and David Welch for their ongoing creative support and collaboration since 2013

endless thanks to Mimi Cirbusova, for her time, vision, and artwork, for bringing to life forces that would otherwise exist in a notebook. I am deeply grateful for your friendship, insight, and talent

to Ryan Rivas at Burrow Press for championing experimental work in publishing, and for his patience and editorial insight

and finally, to Matthew Bailey, for his love, acceptance, and inspiration. I love you nonstop.

ABOUT THE AUTHOR

Avni Vyas is a poet living and writing in Florida. Her poetry and nonfiction can be found in journals such as *Grist*, *Meridian*, *The Pinch*, *Juked*, *Crab Orchard Review*, *Better Magazine*, *Arts and Letters*, *Rigorous Magazine*, and others. With Anne Barngrover, she is the co-author of the chapbook *Candy in Our Brains* (CutBank 2014). She is the Essays editor at *Honey Literary*, and poetry editor at *The Offending Adam*. She teaches in the Writing Program at New College of Florida. You can visit her on Instagram (@singstooloud) and Twitter (@AvniDangerfield).

ABOUT THE ARTIST

Mimi Cirbusova is a creative entrepreneur in Sarasota, Florida. She is the CEO of Meadowsweet Money LLC, where she teaches people how to live a joyful, abundant life on a budget. Mimi is also the co-founder of Compass Rose History Experiences, a female-owned local history company. Her deep connection to native Florida nature can be seen throughout her illustrations and artwork.